What Christians Should Know About…

Power Filled Worship

Russ Hughes

Sovereign World

Copyright © 1999 Russ Hughes

All rights reserved. No part of this publication may be reproduced,
stored in a retrieval system, or transmitted in any form or by any means,
electronic, mechanical, photocopying, recording or otherwise,
without the prior written consent of the publisher.

Short extracts may be quoted for review purposes.

Unless otherwise stated, Scripture quotations are taken from
The Holy Bible, New International Version.
© Copyright 1973, 1978, 1984 International Bible Society.
Used by permission. All rights reserved.

ISBN: 1 85240 267 9

SOVEREIGN WORLD LIMITED
P.O. Box 777, Tonbridge, Kent TN11 0ZS, England.

Typeset and printed in the UK by Sussex Litho Ltd, Chichester, West Sussex.

Contents

1	What's it all about?	5
2	The power of worship	15
3	Capturing a vision and finding a leader	21
4	Some practical help	33

1

What's it all about?

The fight!

The peace of the house was broken by the sound of my five-year-old son and three-year-old daughter bickering. This was a fairly common sound, which often emanates from their bedroom if they are left to play together for any length of time. It would usually come and go over a two-hour period, but this was one of those occasions when it got louder and louder. The crying started, which became screaming and generally sounded more like World War Three, than a child's play session.

I ran up to see what had started this episode – who was playing with whose toy? Who had hit who? To my surprise the answer was more different than I expected. "What's is all this fighting about?" I enquired. Jack, my son went on to explain how they had both started to make something to say how much they loved me, Jack thought crayons were best, Daisy thought paints were even better. This had perpetuated into this full scale fight. Was I hearing Jack correctly? That the reason they were fighting was because they couldn't agree on a way of expressing their love to me?

Sadly, this is an illustration of the scene which we frequently find in our local churches. In our Western consumerist society, we seem to have created a mindset which says that worship is about what we want, how **we** think it should be done. We have endless debates about which style; traditional or modern, catholic or charismatic, organ or band, slow or fast, long or short. God must look down with sadness to see His children fighting over how we express our love to Him!

We recently did a survey of our congregation asking for their responses to our plans for the introduction of four Sunday services instead of the current two. This proposal had been discussed for a number of months amongst the church staff and leadership team. It was then discussed in detail at an away day for our Parochial Church Council, at which we debated over four permutations for the arrangement of the new services. After a great deal of discussion we came to the conclusion that Option 3 would be the most favourable. We conveyed this in the form of a brief report to our congregation and asked five questions to gauge their feelings. On the whole the response was positive and confirmed that both the staff team and the PCC had the support of the congregation.

However, there were some responses which were negative and reflected the point I have already been making. Why can't there be a service that suits me? Why do we have to change? The new arrangements don't fit in with my lifestyle!

Turning to face the Lord

Worship is both giving and receiving, the primary focus of our praise and worship must always be about who God is, what He requires of us. The first commandment given to Moses and reinforced by Jesus expresses this, *'Love the Lord, your God, with all your body, mind and strength.'* God wants our very best, He wants our entire lives given over to Him. John Wimber once said, "worship is the only thing God gets out of the deal!" In other words, He gave us life itself, salvation through the cross and continual blessings on top, all He gets is the worship of His children. God is not another of our consumerist choices, He is to be revered, to be looked to and delighted in.

So what is worship?

In reality, worship defies definition, it's like trying to define love or the taste of a vintage champagne. Just think for a moment trying to define Coca Cola to someone. It's brown, fizzy, has a number of fruity tastes in it and comes in a red can, with a white logo on it. Next time that person goes into a store they may identify a can of Coca Cola, next time they sit in a restaurant they may see a glass of Coca Cola and guess from the description that it is Coca Cola, but does that mean they are any closer to knowing what Coca Cola is like?

Worship is like that. I can give endless descriptions, quote numerous writers on the subject, even get out volumes of theology, however to truly know what worship is we must do it ourselves; we must *"taste and see!"*

In his book *Worship In The Early Church*, Ralph P. Martin gives us this definition:

> *TO WORSHIP GOD IS TO ASCRIBE TO HIM SUPREME WORTH, for He alone is worthy.*[1]

Ordering our priorities

Over the years the conclusion I have reached in this area can be summed up simply by what I call worship priorities:
- Who we worship first
- Why we worship second
- How we worship last.

So many believers seem to have this list turned on its head. God is far less bothered by our outward expression than many of His people are. The Lord looks on the heart.

Who we worship

As Christians we believe a number of things:
- God is creator of all
- God is all powerful – omnipotent
- God is everywhere – omnipresent

---

[1] Ralph P. Martin, WORSHIP IN THE EARLY CHURCH, chapter 1 "The Church – A Worshipping Community," Eerdmands Publishing Company, 1974 revised edition.

- God is all-knowing – omniscient
- God is all-loving. Has always loved us and always will
- God is Saviour, through His Son, Jesus Christ
- God is counsellor, through the person of the Holy Spirit

Are you starting to get the picture? God is almighty, creator of the universe, He can beat anything, be everywhere, know everything, love everyone and has demonstrated this by sending Jesus to save us from our sins. When Jesus left to be with His father, after His death and resurrection, He sent the Holy Spirit to be our comforter, counsellor and empower us for works of grace and mercy.

In her book *Teaching A Stone To Talk*, Annie Dillard wonders if we really know who we come to worship:

> 'Why do we people in churches seem like cheerful, brainless tourists on a packaged tour of the Absolute?... On the whole, I do not find Christians, outside of the catacombs, sufficiently sensible of conditions. Does anyone have the foggiest idea what sort of power we so blithely invoke? Or, as I suspect, does no one believe a word of it? The churches are children playing on the floor with their chemistry sets, mixing up a batch of TNT to kill a Sunday morning. It is madness to wear ladies' straw hats and velvet hats to church; we should all be wearing crash helmets. Ushers should issue life preservers and signal flares; they should lash us to our pews. For the sleeping god (sic) may wake someday and take offence, or the waking god (sic) may draw us out to where we can never return.'

I fear that God will one day take offence, but my prayer is that we will all be drawn into the inner place and return changed forever!

Why we worship

We worship for a number of reasons, two are:

1. We are commanded to do so both in the Old and the New Testament, by God, through Moses and by Jesus himself. (Exodus 20:3 OT and Luke 10: 27 NT)
2. We are inspired to so, through our love for God. (Romans 12:1)

A good way to think about this is in the act of marriage. Am I married to my wife because the law says so, or because I love her? Well the answer is both, as a requirement of the law I took vows of love and faithfulness, both those vows were motivated by my love for her. If I had married my wife just to fulfil a legal requirement without loving her, what kind of marriage would we have? Indeed if I were to rely on the vows which I made some seven years ago, and not continue to express my commitment to our marriage through constant acts of love, what kind of marriage would we have?

For our marriage to be complete we rely on both our fulfilment of the law and our continued acts of love and adoration. Just look at the words of the marriage service:

> The bride and bridegroom face each other.
> The bride and bridegroom takes the bride's right hand in his, and says
>
> I, N, take you, N, to be my wife, to have and to hold from this day forward for better, for worse, for richer, for poorer, in sickness and in health, to love, cherish, and worship, till death us do part, according to God's holy law; and this is my solemn vow.
>
> They loose hands.
> The bride takes the bridegroom's right hand in hers, and says
>
> I, N, take you, N, to be my husband, to have and to hold from this day forward; for better, for worse, for richer, for poorer, in sickness and in health, to love, cherish, and obey, till death us to part, according to God's holy law; and this is

my solemn vow.

© The Central Board of Finance of the Church of England 1980

It is obvious that these words are rich with both love and promises. I find it difficult to understand how any man or woman can utter such words without first considering the implications of making such promises!

We worship God out of obedience to the law *and* out of love for Him, the two go hand in hand. Love and obedience are brothers, not as some would see, enemies. Jesus himself said to his disciples *"If you obey my commands, you will remain in my love."* (John 15:10)

Adoring God

In the church we have to be careful not to forget that people are loved because of who they are and not what they do. God loves us this way; He wants our hearts always before our works. We sometimes forget this of God and our worship can reflect this, thanking God for all the things He has done for us, without worshipping Him for who He is. Let's always remember God's character is worthy of praise in itself.

He is loving, kind, gentle, merciful, gracious, forgiving, righteous, holy and this is just the start! Above all of this God is our Father. As the Spirit of God enters our lives, we know in our hearts that God is Father and this motivates our praise as His children (Romans 8:15-16).

There is a danger when serving the Lord to spend so much time doing the work of the Lord, that we forget the Lord of the work. This has been my own experience and the experience of so many of us in the Church.

We recently staged one of our 'Revival Fire' conferences. We run about three conferences a year to encourage church leaders as we move from renewal to revival. At this particular conference we were privileged to share in ministry with our dear friend Guy Chevreau from the Toronto Airport. From the first evening it was clear what the Lord was calling us to as He broke into our worship with these words, 'Come away with me, my lovely.'

These words flowed from the first to the last moment of the conference. Were we really in love with the Lord? Would we really leave it all behind just to be with Him? Had our works become more important than our relationship? Take a moment to read these words from Song of Songs:

> *My lover is like a gazelle or a young stag.*
> *Look! There he stands behind our wall,*
> *gazing through the windows, peering through the lattice.*
> *My lover spoke and said to me,*
> *"Arise, my darling, my beautiful one, and come with me.*
> *See! The winter is past; the rains are over and gone.*
> *Flowers appear on the earth; the season of singing has come,*
> *the cooing of doves is heard in our land,*
> *The fig-tree forms its early fruit; the blossoming vines spread their fragrance.*
> ***Arise, come, my darling; my beautiful one, come with me."***
> (Proverbs 2:9-13 NIV)

Over the centuries the Song of Songs has caused scholars to have differing opinions on how to interpret it. Many see it as a symbolic representation of Christ's love for His church, the bride of Christ. If this is indeed the case we need to respond to the call to greater intimacy with the Father in worship. The call in these days, as in all that have gone before us, is to be a people in fervent adoration of our God.

The words of this prayer encapsulate just such an act.

> *'I ask you, Lord Jesus, to develop in me, your lover, an immeasurable urge toward you, an affection that is unbounded, a longing that is unrestrained, a fervour that throws discretion to the winds! The more worthwhile our love for you, all the more pressing does it become. Reason cannot hold it in check, fear does not make it tremble, wise*

judgment does not temper it. Amen.'
Richard Rolle (c. 1295–1349)

Adoration is the primary motivation in our worship of God, which can move us into thankful praise. As I write this I am conscious that some may see this as a method for worship. I urge you not to see it is as this. There are times when thankfulness leads us to adoration and I do not wish to create an unbreakable set of rules for worship, because worship is a relational activity.

Thanksgiving

As children both my wife and I were brought up to have good manners. We were always expected to say please and thank you, and now as parents ourselves we too are trying to teach our children the same thing. If you ever hear children praying they will often say please and thank you. Adults, however are not so polite, talking to God in a way which omits to remember that He deserves our utmost respect and reverence.

It is a natural part of any reasonable person's life to say please and thank you, and our worship should be no different. God has so much to be thanked for; for sending Jesus to save us from the destiny of hell and giving us the gift of eternal life with Him in heaven. That's both an act of mercy and of grace; not giving us what we do deserve (Hell), and giving us what we don't deserve (Grace).

Take a moment to think about the cross; an innocent man, spotless, faultless, hanging there in agony. The ultimate humiliation, the curse, strung out for all to see. It took Jesus hours to die, stretched apart, with nails through His wrists and through His feet. His frame hanging as He slowly suffocated, His body weight reducing His ability to breathe. A crown of thorns ripping into His skull, and a back so torn by the blows of the whip that it was bare sinew and flesh dripping with blood. The most barbaric torture known to man, and Jesus the Son of God endured it, although He had committed no crime.

And then, as if there was nothing else to torture this Lamb of

God, every sin committed, from the first one in time until the last, was poured through Him. Every rape, every murder, every act of torture, genocide, infanticide. Every wrong thought, word and action was *'laid upon him.'*

This meant only one thing – that the Father had to look away, He could not bear to look upon the sin – not one second, or even one moment of it. The ultimate pain for Jesus, separation from His Father.

Are you starting to get the picture? The crucifixion, our means of escape, is Jesus on the cross. There is a river of mercy which flows from the throne of God, washing over those who choose to enter into the river. There is only one response, we can make no other. Songs and lives which are full of thanks to God.

We must never forget the cross, it is the ultimate symbol of worship and sacrifice.

The cross would be enough to keep us thankful for eternity, and yet God continues to pour even more upon our lives. The presence of the promised Holy Spirit, acts of grace, healing, mercy and generosity shown to us daily.

We need to start living lives which express thanks to God. In a western society it is very easy to take so much for granted and keep praying for more and more. God wants us to be a people who are grateful, delighting in His goodness and blessing Him as He continually blesses us. The good news is that God wants to give us more than we begin to imagine.

> *"Now to Him who is able to do immeasurably more than all we ask or imagine, according to his power that is at work within us, to him be the glory in the church and in Christ Jesus throughout all generations, for ever and ever! Amen."*
> (Ephesians 3:20-21)

As this first chapter comes to an end ask yourself, "Are my worship priorities in the right order? Do I really understand who God is? Do I really appreciate how much He has done for me? Is He my one desire? Am I delighting in His beauty and His kindness?

Until we get these things worked out, we are in danger of

having "singing lips, but distant hearts" as someone has said. What is it all about? It's about having a passion for God which cannot be contained, pouring out of heartfelt love to the One who truly loves us!

2

The power of worship

Meeting with God

We can never out-give God and worship is no exception. Even though worship is entirely God's and belongs to Him, it is in our acts of worship that God seeks to minister to us. One of the pleasures of leading worship for many years and in many different places is to hear the testimonies which people have shared with me about their own experiences during worship. The stories contained in this chapter should not only amaze us, they should inspire us to expect God to move when we worship Him. The truth that when we draw near to Him, He draws near to us (James 4:8). When God comes near to us we are bound to be changed and as we are transformed He is glorified, this is what it truly means to glorify God in worship. If we come to worship depressed, sick or suffering from any negative condition, and go out again transformed, who gets the glory? God, of course!

If our music and songs are full of spirit and truth, they should have the same effect on people as preaching, teaching, prophecy, healing and deliverance ministries. Now all these ministries are important in their own right and our experience as a congregation is that God uses each of these ministries powerfully. The danger we must guard ourselves against as churches, is thinking that God only speaks words of conviction through preachers, or words of healing through ministry team members, or delivers through deliverance team members. Both the evidence of scripture and in my own experience would say that this view is incorrect.

Dave's story

There are times when we minister and we feel that things could have been much better, and this wet winter's night was one of them. My worship team had been asked to lead worship in a nightclub. It was a new initiative run by the local Youth for Christ and a nightclub, taking over the nightclub for a night and using it for worship, preaching and some dance for young Christians to bring their friends to.

We arrived, set up and played the worship set we had prepared. It felt empty and lacked anointing. It felt wrong, although I was unsure why, as people were singing and worshipping. Perhaps it was the different venue that changed the whole dynamic? We finished, packed up and drove home. This was one event I was happy to forget.

About a year later we ran a baptism evening in church. Just before the service I was approached by a young man. I knew his face but hadn't really ever spoken to him. He told me that he was getting baptized that evening and then proceeded to tell me that I had led him to Christ. I was confused, I didn't know him to talk to and so thought that he might have mistaken me for someone else. I asked him to explain, and this was his story.

It was that night at the club when he had come as a guest. He told me that as the worship was taking place he could see many Christians worshipping God, dancing and singing His praise. He decided to join in for 'the fun of it' and began to jump up and down and sing the songs. As the worship continued he said that the words he was singing started to make sense; not only did they make sense, but he also believed what they said. He went on to tell me how, as he worshipped, he asked Jesus into his life.

There was no talk, no altar call, no ministry time, just the worship. The worship brought both the truth in a way that made sense and in a way that convicted him enough to make a commitment. Was it a valid commitment that lasted? Well, here he was a year on ready to be baptized!

Laura's story

It is often when we feel that we have been least effective, that God has worked in ways which from the outside seem to have been fruitless. Just as with Dave, God had done a deep work which had not been seen on the night; Laura's story again was a lesson in trusting in the Lord and not relying on my own understanding (Proverbs 3:5).

The team was ministering at a conference and the evening was coming to a close. The speaker had finished and the ministry team had come forward to pray with those who were responding to God. One of my team, Meg, had been encouraged for about a year previously to move out in the prophetic. On a number of occasions she had been told that she had a prophetic gift and should use it. One day she came to me and said that people kept telling her to prophesy and what should she do. I thought the answer was obvious so said 'have you thought of prophesying?'

As we were leading the worship during ministry I felt that this was the night that the Lord wanted Meg to step out in faith, to sing out words from the heart of God over those being prayed for. I encouraged Meg to do this. She started; Meg who had no problem with confidence or projection was different this time, her words were quiet like a mouse and un-confident. As she sang tears poured down her face and within a matter of minutes her attempt to sing out prophetically was over. She left the platform, looking somewhat disturbed.

After the meeting I went and spoke with her. She was crying and said that it was not the right time, that she was not ready and needed to wait longer. I felt awful, I went home feeling just as disturbed. Had I got it wrong? Had I let my enthusiasm get the better of me? Had I forced Meg into doing something which she was not ready for? Had I presumed on the Lord? I had a sleepless night as these thoughts went through my mind. The next morning I took Meg aside and apologised.

About a week later I was sitting in church and was approached by Laura. We chatted for some time and then as she got up to leave she said, 'Oh, I forgot to tell you.' She continued, 'When I was at the Revival Fire conference I was being prayed for. The ministry team were praying for me and felt that it was getting nowhere. But when Meg started to sing it was like a key turned and the prayer took effect.' As you can imagine I was filled with joy, both for Laura and for Meg. I encouraged Laura to tell Meg as soon as she could and she did. Every one of us was encouraged, most of all Meg. To her, the offering she brought was weak and helpless, but as the inspired word of God it was filled with the power to bring healing.

Jenny's story

I am so privileged to share in the lives of so many people as I minister. The wonderful thing about ministry is knowing that God is using us to change lives for eternity. He allows us to share in His sovereign work. Jenny's story for me is one which brings tears to my eyes each time I recall it.

It was a Sunday evening service and at the end of the service I was introduced to Jenny who had been a visitor to our service on this occasion. She had been visibly moved during the worship and tears had not stopped flowing throughout the evening. I was asked if I would speak and pray with her and agreed to do so with another member of the ministry team.

'I know I shouldn't have come' she cried. 'I don't believe in God or anything, but I have just cried all night.' We listened and I tried to explain that it was probably the Holy Spirit despite Jenny not believing in God.

We spent some time listening and talking and finding out about her circumstances. She told us of her loneliness and of her need for someone special. I asked her if I could pray for anything that she would want. 'A man,' she said. Well if that's what she really wanted it was no good me praying for something else, so we prayed that God would hear her cry and answer this prayer. She left, not having made a commitment.

Some weeks later she was back in church and still visibly moved by the service. At the end I went to talk with her. 'How are you?' I asked. 'I did something really stupid,' she said. She went on to tell me that she had got a man, a married man! This was not the answer I was hoping for. She continued. As expected the whole relationship had gone horribly wrong. He would not leave his wife and in the process Jenny had lost all her friends, who had sided with this man's wife. She continued, 'so I decided to kill myself.' She told of how she had taken pills and written a letter to her mother explaining her actions. However as she was dying she re-read the letter and spotted a spelling mistake. For whatever reason this brought her back to her senses and she called her sister and told her she was dying. Within minutes she was in hospital undergoing treatment.

A few days later her father arrived to see her. 'I will give you anything you want, just tell me and I will do it,' he said in desperation. Her request was a simple one, 'take me back to that church in Maidstone.' Here she was again telling me the story, but this time it was different. We prayed and she asked Jesus into her life.

A number of months later she returned to our church for the baptism of her nephew. She took the brave step of sharing this story with her whole family and with our church. I will never forget the last thing she said as she closed her testimony. 'I'm not lonely anymore.'

Ministry can often have many disappointments. We can be discouraged, disillusioned and feel like giving up at times, thinking that our contribution is useless. When I start to think like this I remind myself of Jenny, lost and lonely, helpless and searching, but now transformed by the love of Jesus, through the power of worship.

Bob's story

I was on a trip to the United States and leading worship at a mission. After the meeting a biker approached me. 'I want a word with you' he said. I thought that I might have offended him with something I sang or said!

We went to a quiet place in the meeting. 'Do you know,' he said, 'during that meeting tonight as the worship was going on, God was performing open heart surgery on me. He was dealing with some really deep hurts.' He finished and hugged me.

The evidence as I travel and minister gets greater as each story is shared with me, that as we worship God and as the music is played and the word of God is proclaimed through song, He moves in the lives of individuals. He brings salvation, healing, deliverance and words of prophecy, people are changed by His power.

I wonder what you expect to happen when you worship in your church? Do you expect God to minister to His people through the music and song? Do you expect people to be changed? Do you look for salvation without preaching and healing without prayer? This should not be the exception when we worship but the norm. As we pour our hearts out in worship to God, He pours His mercy and grace upon us. I pray this will be your experience and the experience of your church.

3

Capturing a vision and finding a leader

A note to the reader

Much of what is talked about in this chapter is aimed at church leaders. This is because in order for any church-based ministry to be effective it must be within the whole vision of the church, owned by it's leadership and subject to their authority. However, you will still be able to appreciate the principles written about which need to be understood by both leaders, and those under their authority.

Vision

All effective ministry starts with a vision, in fact all great things start with a vision. Henry Ford had a vision of making the car affordable to every American, and from this vision came the Model T Ford and today, one of the world's biggest automotive manufacturers. A man called Neil Armstrong looked up at the moon and dreamed of going there; he became the first man on the moon. In the 1970's a young man by the name of Bill Hybels listened as an inspirational teacher talked and fuelled a dream of a church that functioned just like the early church in Acts. Today Bill Hybels is Senior Pastor of the church that the dream started with, the Willow Creek Church, with some 15,000 members.

Nehemiah had a vision, to see the walls of Jerusalem rebuilt and the honour of Israel restored. With that vision he gathered a team and we read that they began the rebuilding together, and the dream became reality.

If you want power filled worship that changes people in your church, you must capture that vision. Worship that seeks God's face before His hand, worship which gives God space to speak and time for those listening to respond. Worship that moves away from the written words and scores and sings and plays prophetically from the father-heart of God. Worship which is for an audience of one, seeking to please God and not the opinions of the people. Worship which is dangerous and exciting, which is more like a white rapid ride than a rowing trip. This is a direction which requires vision. Why? Because it means:

1. Your leadership must want to go down this road
2. Dealing with the misunderstanding and criticism of others
3. Moving into places which you have never been to before
4. Getting a leader and a team who share in this vision
5. Developing your gifts to move in this way.

There are times when things get so tough that the only thing we are sure of is that God has given us a vision and He will fulfil it.

I believe we are living in a time when God is raising up worship leaders who will sing and play out the songs of His heart, not just the odd one here and there, but a whole generation. Many churches are reporting the move of the prophetic within their worship. We for one, are hearing more and more from God during our worship, and although we still plan our worship in detail, often those plans are changed as the Spirit leads us to take a different direction during the meeting.

The challenge

As leaders are you prepared to go this way? It means trust in God rather than the paper list you have before you. It means stepping out of your liturgy at times. It means communicating with your people as to why you believe this way of worship is vital for you as you move in renewal. It means selecting those to lead your worship, who exhibit the sensitivity and maturity to move in this way. It also means trusting them, sometimes without notice.

Establishing and releasing authority

I am part of a leadership team which is part of the Church of England. There are three of us, the Vicar, Associate Minister and myself, the Director of Music. In the structures of the Church of England the Vicar works out of the authority of the Bishop. He is given many charges, but one of them is to direct the worship of the people. This of course is meant in it's widest sense, however whilst he has overall authority and control in our services, he chooses to allow me, under this authority to minister in this way. This is vital, as his trust and encouragement enable me to move out prophetically, knowing that he believes in this vision and trusts me to lead us in it.

Different denominations have different ways of leading and authority flows in varying ways. However, as senior leaders of your church, the buck will always stop with you in every area. If you already have a worship leader you must give him the authority to move in this way. If you don't trust him to do this then you need to ask why. If you cannot trust him, why is he doing this job? You will of course need to set out some ground rules that both of you understand fully in order to guard against misunderstanding and conflict. You will need to share this vision and ensure that he can capture it. Is he equipped for this role? Does he exhibit prophetic insight, spiritual sensitivity, maturity and authority? As I said, trying to take your church down this road may give you more problems than answers, which is why it has to be built on a vision; one that says what you are trying to do and why.

Only this week I have been speaking to one such leader who has captured a vision to renew his church's worship. He is facing awful criticism, both verbal and written. Some members of his church have left, others remain in the body, but continue to oppose him. He is upset by this and shaken, yet firm in his resolve to move forward for the sake of the gospel. Are you prepared, just as Nehemiah was, to take on a task which will bring it's critics, opponents and even enemies from within?

The vision helps people decide

On the wall of my office there are many things; scripture quotes, funny cartoons but two very important documents, our church vision and my worship vision. They are there for two reasons; to remind me and to explain to others where we are heading.

When people come to see me about joining the worship ministry of our church I take them through the worship vision step by step and explain to them each part of it. I also have evenings for the whole team where we look through it together, after which I ask them this question, 'do you believe it and can you follow it?' If they can then they are able to take part in this ministry, if not, then I ask them to think seriously about joining or staying.

This may seem a little harsh, however I believe that the vision we have for worship has been given to us by God. I have authority to lead this ministry and for the foreseeable future I do not plan to change this vision. The only thing that could result from having people in this ministry who don't share the vision would be harm. At some point they would want to go in a direction that the vision clearly doesn't, or in fact not go in a way we believe we should. This can only lead to unnecessary conflict and I have to protect the ministry from that.

Having met couples who are discussing the idea of having children some years into their marriage and finding then out that one of them wants children and the other doesn't, is heartbreaking. This should have been discussed and resolved before marriage took place and avoiding much heartbreak and pain.

On such fundamental issues of purpose and direction, ministry is the same. Don't get me wrong, we still have discussions and even disagreements about certain things, but we all share the same vision and want the same things for our ministry, and ultimately the extension of God's kingdom and His glory.

Leadership

This leads me on to my next point; all vision must be led. There must be one person who will capture this vision and take it forward, who will take the responsibility of seeing the vision become reality. The Bible gives us clear models – Moses, Joshua, Nehemiah, and Paul, to name just four, all people determined to help fulfil the purposes of God for their generation.

There are a number of things to look for in your leader:

They must be a Christian and filled with the Holy Spirit

It may seem a little obvious, but I must say this, if you are expecting this leader to worship in spirit and truth and lead others in this way, they must know the truth of the Bible. They must have accepted Jesus as their personal Saviour and be filled with the Holy Spirit and have experience of ministering in power. It goes without saying that when we give our lives to Christ we receive His Holy Spirit, however Paul encourages us to go on being filled. Once was never God's plan, to 'be filled' is an ongoing process. In the original Greek text, the tense is a perfect one and can be literally translated as 'be filled', 'go on being filled'. *'Do not get drunk on wine, which leads to debauchery. Instead, be filled with the Spirit.'* (Romans 5:18)

Have a worshipper's heart

> *'I will praise you, O LORD, with all my heart; I will tell of all your wonders.'* (Psalm 9:1)

A good worship leader is nothing more than a worshipper who leads. This may sound a little simplistic, but when I look for those to lead worship within our congregation I look for worshippers who have leadership potential, rather than leaders who have worship potential. Worship flows from the heart and cannot be taught, whereas leadership skills can be developed and taught.

Competence for the task

> *'Kenaniah the head Levite was in charge of the singing; that was his responsibility because he was skilful at it.'*
> (1 Chronicles 15:22)

It is not enough just to have a worshipper's heart; there are many who love to praise the Lord but lack the ability to sing or play an instrument. In Chronicles we read that Kenaniah was chosen because he was skilful. There are many reasons why people are in ministry, and sometimes they are wrong ones. Perhaps they believe that is where God wants them, although they exhibit no gifting. Sometimes people minister because no one else will do it. Perhaps it's because they have always done it and their mother before them. These are not good reasons for Christian service. All ministry must flow out of a desire to serve the body with the gifts that God has given us, in the area we are passionate about. I have been very impressed with the Network Program developed by the Willow Creek Church, helping believers to discover where they belong in the body of Christ, using this principle. 'The right people, in the right places, for the right reasons.'

Your worship leaders must be good at what they do. God deserves the very best we can bring. Poor musicianship and singing are not the best we can bring. Now as I write I know some of you will be struggling with limited people resources and the only person you have has limited skills. If this is the case and you are serious about giving God the best, get them lessons in playing or singing. Send them on worship courses and conferences, invest in the making of a leader. It will be money well spent!

In our church we have the blessing of many musicians and singers, of varying skills and ability. For this reason we have set up a structure that helps those with limited skills to develop both their competence and experience. We have different areas of ministry, not just Sunday services, and people get to use their gifts in an area which is appropriate to their level of competence. Many people could handle leading worship with guitar in a small group, but not all could handle a celebration of 500 people. We are in danger of hindering people's growth by putting them into areas of ministry which they may fall in, and so discourage them for the future. I like to think of it like learning to fly. When a student begins they start in a small single prop plane with an instructor by their side, not on their own in a 747.

Spiritual maturity, authority and sensitivity

> '*He must not be a recent convert, or he may become conceited and fall under the same judgment as the devil. He must also have a good reputation with outsiders, so that he will not fall into disgrace and into the devil's trap. Deacons, likewise, are to be men worthy of respect, sincere, not indulging in much wine, and not pursuing dishonest gain. They must keep hold of the deep truths of the faith with a clear conscience.*' (1 Timothy 3:6-9)

Here we read some common sense teaching on the appointment of leaders. If they are a recent convert they may become conceited, or in other words the power may go to their heads. We have a responsibility as leaders not to allow this to happen to new converts. In practical terms I would expect any leader to have walked with the Lord for at least three years. Has this person walked faithfully with the Lord both in the good and the bad times? Are they regular attendee's of church? Is their personal life exhibiting the lordship of Christ, in their handling of money, their family, their conduct? It is also important to say that there are those in their late teens who show spiritual maturity and those in their 60's who are immature. Spiritual maturity does not necessarily equate to the age of a believer.

Authority flows from having the respect of others, gained through exhibiting maturity. Leadership without authority is impotent, people will not listen or follow. Look around your church, who do people follow? You may be surprised to find that it may not be those who are currently known as leaders. It may be those without the leadership titles. Titles are worthless in the Kingdom of God, it is testimony that counts. God is not impressed by the titles we give ourselves, He is more interested in who we are and what we do, rather than who we say we are and what we say we will do.

Spiritual sensitivity comes from having walked with the Lord for some time, learning to hear His voice and understand His prompting. Discerning His ways and knowing His heart, learning to understand what pleases Him and makes Him angry. What delights Him and what makes Him sad. Jesus exhibited spiritual sensitivity. *'The one who sent me is with me; he has not left me alone, for I always do what pleases him."* (John 8:29) Look at the ministry of Jesus, the model for all who seek to be sensitive to the Father.

Prophetic insight

This is particularly important for those wishing to move in power filled worship. Learning to know where God is leading, and hearing what is on His heart for a congregation is imperative if we are to lead people into intimate worship. There have been many occasions when we have planned to take one direction within a service and the Lord has taken us in another way. We came to celebrate and the Lord wanted us to repent. Sometimes there may be those in a congregation who need to hear a word from God, and He will break into our worship and cause us to sing out the words. We need to have the eyes of the eagle, soaring in worship and seeing from those heavenly places.

The character of a leader

If one thing can spoil anointing it is poor character. Character plays an important part in leadership and particularly in the area of worship leading where one has to keep in check the reasons why one is doing the ministry. This area of ministry has it's own temptations, fame, acclaim, the attention of those who may be attracted to our gifts, the desire to perform, to name just a few. Those embarking on this ministry must face them head on, look out for the temptation and resist it. Ministry is as much about who we become as it is what we do. Remember that God is preparing us for heaven and making us more like Jesus, not just using us to do a job. (2 Corinthians 3:18)

Here are four character indicators to look for:

Able to submit to authority

Is this person able to submit to authority? Do they recognize that they minister with your permission and blessing? Do they have the same vision as you for the church? Do they know the boundaries in which they minister? Will they stay within those boundaries? The answer to all these questions must be yes, otherwise you will have problems on your hands. Now we all know that there are leaders who seem to thrive on power and each one of us must examine ourselves to ensure that we also are working under authority and open to submission. One of the joys of the team I belong to is that although there is a structure of leadership, we all submit to one another in love. There has never been an occasion where harsh leadership or overbearing power has been exercised. Your leadership must flow out of love, which in turn will result in those under you submitting to you out of love, rather than fear.

> '*Submit to one another out of reverence for Christ.*'
> (Ephesians 5:21)

Be open to correction
One of the signs of true humility is one who remains teachable and open to correction. As we experiment with the structure of services, the ways in which we worship, the gifts we exercise, we are bound to make mistakes. Those who wish to move out in the prophetic must be open to correction, for at times they too will make mistakes. These may be incorrect or unanointed prophecy, or incorrect timing within a service. All prophets must remember they are human and imperfect and will get things wrong.

> '*For we know in part and we prophesy in part, but when perfections comes, the imperfect disappears.*'
> (1 Corinthians 13:9-10)

Living in holiness
It is true that God uses cracked pots, but not dirty ones. Whilst our reputation relies on what is seen by people in public, our walk with the Lord is measured not only by our public acts but also our private acts and thoughts. We must remain holy in order to maintain a right relationship with God, our Father. Our priority must be to maintain intimacy with the Lord and sin destroys this.

My own experience has been that when I have had unconfessed sin within my heart I am unable to truly minister with kingdom authority and power. We need to learn to keep short accounts with God and with each other.

Able to face failure
All ministry has it's share of success and failure and this one is no exception. I could write a separate book with stories of my own failure, starting songs in the wrong key, forgetting words, unanointed prophecy and inappropriate timing. What encourages me is that the Bible is full of failures used by God to do mighty works. The important thing is that leaders learn from their mistakes and carry on undeterred in their desire to fulfil the task that God has given them. Look for those with a fighting spirit, who will not dwell on their past mistakes, but on God's promises. These people fulfil visions!

> *'Not that I have already obtained all this, or have already been made perfect, but I press on to take hold of that for which Christ Jesus took hold of me. Brothers, I do not consider myself yet to have taken hold of it. But one thing I do: Forgetting what is behind and straining towards the goal to win the prize for which God has called me heavenwards in Christ Jesus.'* Philippians 3:9

Anointed and appointed

I have the privilege of working with other churches and helping them to develop a vision for their worship. One thing I make very clear is the need for a leader to take the worship vision forward. Some have taken this advice and others have chosen not to. The result has been clear; without a leader very little is achieved, and in some cases although the intention was there from the start, without someone to own and take the vision forward very little gets done and very little change occurs.

The second problem is those church leaders who have asked someone to lead this ministry, but have not publicly appointed them for the task. It is not enough for you to select a leader and ask them to get on with it. The church family need to know that this person is appointed to have authority in this area, otherwise there is every chance that their effectiveness will be limited by misunderstanding and arguments about who is leading this area of the church's ministry. If you sincerely believe that they are the right person for the task announce it to your church with joy and excitement. Tell them that he or she is leading under your authority and that this area of ministry is under their direction. Ask them to come to the front of church and ask others to lay hands on them and commission them for this area of service. If you take these steps, the chances of misunderstanding about authority and responsibility are minimized.

Whatever ministry teams you set up within your churches, the leaders you select must be both anointed and appointed. There are many things that exasperate me about the Church of England, however, they have clear models for this principle. When a priest has completed his training there is a service of ordination, at which the Bishop lays his hands on each candidate. By doing so he anoints them for their calling and appoints them to minister under his authority.

A clear principle adopted in the first church, of anointing and appointing those for ministry is found in the book of Acts:

> *"In those days when the number of disciples was increasing, the Grecian Jews among them complained against the Hebraic Jews because their widows were being overlooked in the daily distribution of food. So the Twelve gathered all the disciples together and said, 'It would not be right for us to neglect the ministry of the word of God in order to wait on tables. Brothers, choose seven men from among you who are known to be full of the Spirit and wisdom. We will turn this responsibility over to them and will give our attention to prayer and the ministry of the word.' This proposal pleased the whole group. They chose Stephen, a man full of faith and of the Holy Spirit; also Philip, Procorus, Nicanor, Timon, Parmenas, and Nicolas from Antioch, a convert to Judaism. They presented these men to the apostles, who prayed and*

laid their hands on them." Acts 6:1-6

Pray for the Lord to give you a vision for worship which brings you a new understanding of who He is, enabling your church to hear His voice through the worship of the saints. Find the person who can lead the vision and share the load with you, anoint and appoint them, light the blue touch paper then stand back!

4

Some practical help

When I set out to write this book, I wanted not only to inspire and encourage those who read it, but equip them too. I have read many books which have made me want to move more in the power of God, but I have not always been directed into the practical steps for making this happen.

In this final chapter I want to talk about the principles with which our ministry is built. In doing this I'm not saying we have all the answers, or that this is the only way, rather that these ways have been helpful to our ministry. I also want to make it quite clear that all works of God are initiated by Him and we can't create formulas which guarantee success in ministry, we certainly can't create them to initiate a response from God. What you are about to read are principles based upon the scriptures. Adapt them to fit your needs and structures, and I hope that they help you to move in power filled worship.

Building a team

Nehemiah had a vision to rebuild the walls, but we read that he gathered a team around him and that they began the good work together. *"Let us start the rebuilding, So they began this good work."* (Nehemiah 2:18)

Teams are a God-given gift; they inspire, encourage, challenge and most of all they help us with the work. I would not be able to fulfil the vision I have for the ministry within St. Luke's without the team I have; musicians, singers, sound operators, OHP operators and intercessors. Each one of these people makes a significant contribution to the worshipping life of our church.

How do we select the team? With the following criteria; they must be:
- A Christian and filled with the Holy Spirit
- Signed up to the worship vision
- Competent for the task
- Able to submit to the leadership and the team in love
- Open to varying styles
- Teachable
- Committed to excellence

Much of the above I have talked about in the previous chapter. As you can see many of the criteria for team members are the same as those which are expected of the leader.

Getting them involved

As people emerge who show interest in the worship ministry or who we feel exhibit potential in this area we use practical ways of testing their calling.

1. I spend some time with them, explaining the vision and the principles of the ministry. We also spend some time getting to know one another.

2. They are invited to take part in a service. This give us the chance to listen to them and see how they operate in a worship team. One thing to bear in mind is that usually the first time can be a little daunting and they can be nervous, so we have to be careful not to be too harsh in our judgement.

3. We then talk afterwards to see how they felt about things. Often this gives us the opportunity to talk a little more about specifics such as what they enjoyed doing and what they found difficult.

4. At this stage if both sides feel happy about things, then we will agree to a commitment to the ministry for a period such

as 6 months. This period should give both sides the opportunity to test the calling and see if the ministry is for them.

These four practical steps allow us to test what God is saying to us about each person who comes into the ministry. It may seem very official, however it is meant to help us to test things in stages, and allows those who want to try out this ministry to do so without making too much of a commitment.

One thing about commitment, we do not allow people who wish to 'have a go' at worship now and again to be involved. We want people to take their commitment to this ministry seriously and see it as a ministry rather than 'another thing' to do in church. Many people like to sing in the shower, or tinker about on the piano, however this does not necessarily mean that they are called to be involved in a worship ministry – worship is more than just music!

Bars of soap

Whilst we take commitment seriously, we have to recognize that on the whole our teams are made up of volunteers. People who are giving up their time to serve God in this way. Many have busy lives, jobs, partners and children to name just a few. For this reason we try and exercise flexibility with our teams. If someone is unable to make it then we accept it. We don't make them feel guilty; we thank them for telling us and tell them to have a good time as they fufil their other commitments.

Recently members of the team have had busy work schedules, family commitments, births and deaths to cope with. If these occur we will suggest that they take some time out of the ministry until things are better and they feel able to return.

God has been faithful to us in His provision of people and we have been blessed by new worship leaders and varying types of musicians just at the right time. Volunteers are like bars of soap, if we try to squeeze them too hard then we have every chance of losing them. If at the start you have tested their calling and commitment you should not be afraid to let go from time to time.

Working together

Each worship band we use at St. Luke's is what we call a Core Team. Each Core Team is a set of musicians who work together all the time. We have five teams and five worship leaders, who work with different Core Teams at different times. Core Teams have the following benefits:
- Teams work together on a regular basis and therefore create the relational dynamic which helps all good teams to work effectively.
- No person is overused or underused.
- People are aware when they are needed.
- Worship leaders don't have to worry about finding a team.

When teams work together for any length of time they start to understand one another, as people and as musicians. It is important that we get to know one another, because as we work together, we grow in love, respect, submission, and we encourage one another. No one is trying to score points, or trying to be clever, I am thrilled in the way each of our teams has individuals who are working for the good of the team. There is nothing more destructive in worship than to have musicians trying to be clever, or the loudest, or the best singer. The platform is not a place for competition, it is a place for humility. They are however striving for excellence as they sing and play, knowing that God delights in our excellence. It is what He deserves. I use the word excellence, rather than perfection, remembering that God expects our best, not perfection!

Encouraging creativity

As people join the team they often will ask how would I like them to sing or play? Anyone who has worked with me for any length of time will know that I am very clear about what I do and don't like, however it is much better to give people the ability to express themselves, rather than giving your own opinions.

Creativity comes out of freedom of expression and we need to create safe, encouraging environments for people to try out ideas. You are far more likely to release creativity in this way, rather than trying to impose your own ideas. I find myself constantly thrilled by the ideas that different instrumentalists and singers come up with during our rehearsals and within the worship itself. There may be times when some ideas don't work, however the rich contributions that come in an environment of freedom are worth paying this small cost.

If a musician or singer does do something that is not in keeping with the song, or more of a distraction than an aid to worship, speak with them privately afterwards or next time you meet. Don't make a big deal about it, be gentle, for if you are too harsh you may crush them and the creativity they bring. The benefit of working with the same musicians on a regular basis is that there is a sensitivity to where we are going with a particular song, or even more importantly where the Lord may be leading us.

Choosing the material

I know that each person uses different ways of choosing material for worship. We are all wired differently and some worship leaders spend hours or in some cases days selecting songs. I am not one of those people.

Do we follow a thematic path and choose songs to fit in with the theme of the service? I am personally not convinced that our minds function in this way during worship. Worship is about a spiritual journey into the presence of God, not a multimedia showcase of similar ideas. However it is helpful during certain seasons to give worshippers songs which are familiar, such as Christmas and Easter, but be creative. Find out what God is saying to the World Church. Find out what God is saying to your church through prayer and consultation with leaders and intercessors. Then ask God, "What do You want to say today?"

I pray and ask God to give me insight into where He may want to take the congregation on this occasion. Is it a day to celebrate, or to repent? Are the people hurting or seeking to express their thanksgiving? With this insight I will then select songs which I believe will help us on this journey. I also take a selection of other material in case I have misheard the Lord and He leads us in a different path during the worship.

Expecting the unexpected

If we are to move in freedom during worship we must be prepared for this, we pray, plan, practice, and rehearse hard to ensure that even in our freedom we still are able to give our best. This is not a case of let go and let God, there is no substitute for preparation. Chaos in the name of freedom, because we didn't prepare, is no excuse!

At each rehearsal the team will rehearse the songs which may appear during the service. Remember these musicians and singers are working together regularly so they are sensitive to each other and to the Lord.

Once the rehearsal is over we take some time to be with the Lord and pray for insight, for the release of worship and for Him to lead us as we worship, for the Holy Spirit is the best worship leader we have!

During the service we have before us a running order of songs, plus those in reserve. On some occasions we stay with the order, on others we step out of it. There are occasions when we give up with running orders altogether. God's plan is different!

The unseen worship team

So far I have talked about those who minister from the platform, however this is just a small part of the whole team who help in the ministry of worship within our church.

The intercessors
We have a small team who intercede specifically for the worship

ministry. They have a passion for worship and the gift of intercession. They cover the church, the ministry, the team and myself in prayer. I can't stress how essential this team is to the ministry. They pray for protection, insight, the release of the Holy Spirit. They bring words from the Lord and help me as I seek to discover what season we may be in and how the Lord may be wanting to lead us. They pray to break the strongholds of the enemy as he attempts to disrupt the worship of God and to discourage us as we seek to worship the Lord. If you haven't got a group like this make it a priority to set one up!

The sound team
The aim of all worship leading is to encourage believers to worship God and to remove all distractions which would hinder this. Good sound systems and sound operators are another essential component in the worship ministry. If the sound is of poor quality or not operated in a way which is helpful, either too loud or quiet, then this will be a distraction. Again God has blessed us with a great sound team, led by a leader who is passionate about worship and committed to achieving good sound in worship. The team all have servant hearts and seek to bless the church with this gift.

When we rehearse, the first thing we do is ensure that our fold-back monitors are set correctly. Can everybody hear themselves and each other? Can everybody hear the leader? We do this for two reasons:
1. If the band can hear everything clearly, they will be able to relax and get on with the job. It also means we can get on with the rehearsal.
2. Once we are rehearsing, the sound operator can carry on adjusting the balance for the congregation without holding up the rehearsal time.

The sound check is vital and should always be given priority. Remember that sound operators should be encouraged to express creativity, trying different balances for different songs, or perhaps adding more reverb to the vocal in a quieter song. They should be encouraged to be more than just "caretakers" in this role.

The OHP/Projector team

Most churches are using OHP's for their song words today, some are now moving on to computers with video projectors. Again it is essential that worshippers can see and read the words to the songs and that they appear at the right time. As you can imagine the operators need to be flexible as the songs may change during a service. St. Luke's is again blessed with operators who have servant hearts and show a willingness to be flexible. You need to find people who have these character traits and don't get stressed by change – they also have to be able to concentrate as the songs change, or if songs are repeated.

I know I have said it already but do not underestimate the need for effective ministry in these three areas. All people serving in these areas need to share the worship vision and be committed to it, exercising their individual gifts in order to help achieve it.

Checklist

You may find it helpful to use this checklist as you prepare for worship.

- Pray – Confess your sins, worship the Lord, ask for His insight and inspiration.
- Choose your songs
- Meet the band to rehearse with enough time to practice and prepare
- Set up and tune up
- Do the soundcheck – make sure you can all hear
- Pray together
- Rehearse the songs, developing new ideas, etc
- Finish the rehearsal, say, 30 minutes before the meeting. This will give you time to relax, visit the toilet, get your music in order, etc.
- Spend time praying before the service
- Lead the worship – worship God and encourage others to do the same
- At the end of the meeting, leaders thank the team
- Thank God

- Go and relax!

I am aware as this book comes to an end that much of it has been practical, I do not apologize for this. In some quarters the task of leading worship has been over-spiritualized at the expense of practical preparation, some have the attitude that as long as we are sincere then that's all that matters. I believe that worship is a spiritual activity, however it can be spoilt by the distractions of poor planning, unskilled musicianship, and other distractions such as poor sound and visual aids.

Let us consider how we can do our best as leaders, musicians, singers, sound and video operators in order to minimize distractions in worship. Our prayer is that we become transparent and God is seen in all His glory.

In closing

We were created to worship, it is all that we are going to be doing in heaven. Are you preparing for heaven or not? If you are a leader are you preparing your people for heaven?

Capture the vision, seek the Lord with all your heart, encourage each one to do the same. Go into the inner place, for it is there we meet with Almighty God and in doing so are transformed forever!

I leave you with this vision, it is my sincere prayer and desire for all of us to experience the presence of the Lord as did those early priests.

> 'All the priests who were there consecrated themselves, regardless of their divisions. All the Levites who were musicians – Asaph, Heman, Juduthun and their sons and relatives – stood on the east side of the altar, dressed in fine linen and playing cymbals, harps and lyres. They were accompanied by 120 priests sounding trumpets. The trumpets and singers joined in unison, as with one voice, to give praise and thanks to the Lord. Accompanied by trumpets, cymbals and other instruments, they raise their voices in praise to the Lord and sang:

"He is good; his love endures forever."
Then the temple of the Lord was filled with a cloud, and the priests could not perform their because of the cloud, for the glory of the Lord filled the temple of God.'

2 Chronicles 5:11-14

Other titles available in the 'What Christians Should Know About...' series:

Depression, Anxiety, Mood Swings and Hyperactivity
By Dr. Grant Mullen

The Endtime Harvest
By David Shibley

Escaping From Debt
By Keith Tondeur

Generational Sin
By Pennant Jones

The Glory of God
By Ed Roebert

How to Pray Effectively for Your Lost Loved Ones
By David Alsobrook

The Importance of Forgiveness
By John Arnott

A Personal Relationship with God
By Peter Nodding

Preparing for Christ's Return
By Clive Corfield

Reconciliation
By John Dawson

Sickness and Healing
By Ed Harding

Power Filled Worship
By Russ Hughes

❖ ❖ ❖ ❖

If you have enjoyed this book and would like to help us to send a copy of it and many other titles to needy pastors in the **Third World**, please write for further information or send your gift to:

Sovereign World Trust, P.O. Box 777, Tonbridge, Kent TN11 0ZS, United Kingdom

or to the **'Sovereign World'** distributor in your country.